BLOCKBUSTERS

THE MAKING OF TOY STORY

KENNY ABDO

Fly!
An Imprint of Abdo Zoom
abdobooks.com

abdobooks.com

Published by Abdo Zoom, a division of ABDO, P.O. Box 398166, Minneapolis, Minnesota 55439.

Printed in the United States of America, North Mankato, Minnesota.
052023
092023

THIS BOOK CONTAINS
RECYCLED MATERIALS

Photo Credits: Alamy, Everett Collection, Getty Images, Shutterstock
Production Contributors: Kenny Abdo, Jennie Forsberg, Grace Hansen
Design Contributors: Candice Keimig, Neil Klinepier, Colleen McLaren

Library of Congress Control Number: 2022946932

Publisher's Cataloging-in-Publication Data

Names: Abdo, Kenny, author.
Title: The making of Toy Story / by Kenny Abdo
Description: Minneapolis, Minnesota : Abdo Zoom, 2024 | Series: Blockbusters | Includes online resources and index.
Identifiers: ISBN 9781098281335 (lib. bdg.) | ISBN 9781098282035 (ebook) | ISBN 9781098282387 (Read-to-me ebook)
Subjects: LCSH: Motion pictures--Juvenile literature. | Filmmaking (Motion pictures)--Juvenile literature. | Toy story (Motion picture)--Juvenile literature. | Motion pictures--Production and direction--Juvenile literature.
Classification: DDC 791.43--dc23

TABLE OF CONTENTS

TOY STORY

Following the adventures of Buzz Lightyear and Woody made *Toy Story* a movie audiences loved to play over and over!

Released in 1995, *Toy Story* was the first fully computer-animated movie ever made.

Getting the groundbreaking film to the big screen was a difficult task.

LIGHTS, CAMERA, ...

The company Pixar started out selling computer **hardware**. To show off its products, Pixar made short films. *Tin Toy* was released in 1988.

It was directed by John Lasseter. *Tin Toy* won the Best Short Film **Academy Award**.

After the win, Disney asked Pixar to make a feature-length film. Lasseter, inspired by the toys of his childhood, **pitched** the idea for *Toy Story*. Disney loved the idea. So, with the studio behind them and the idea in place, production began in 1993.

ACTION!

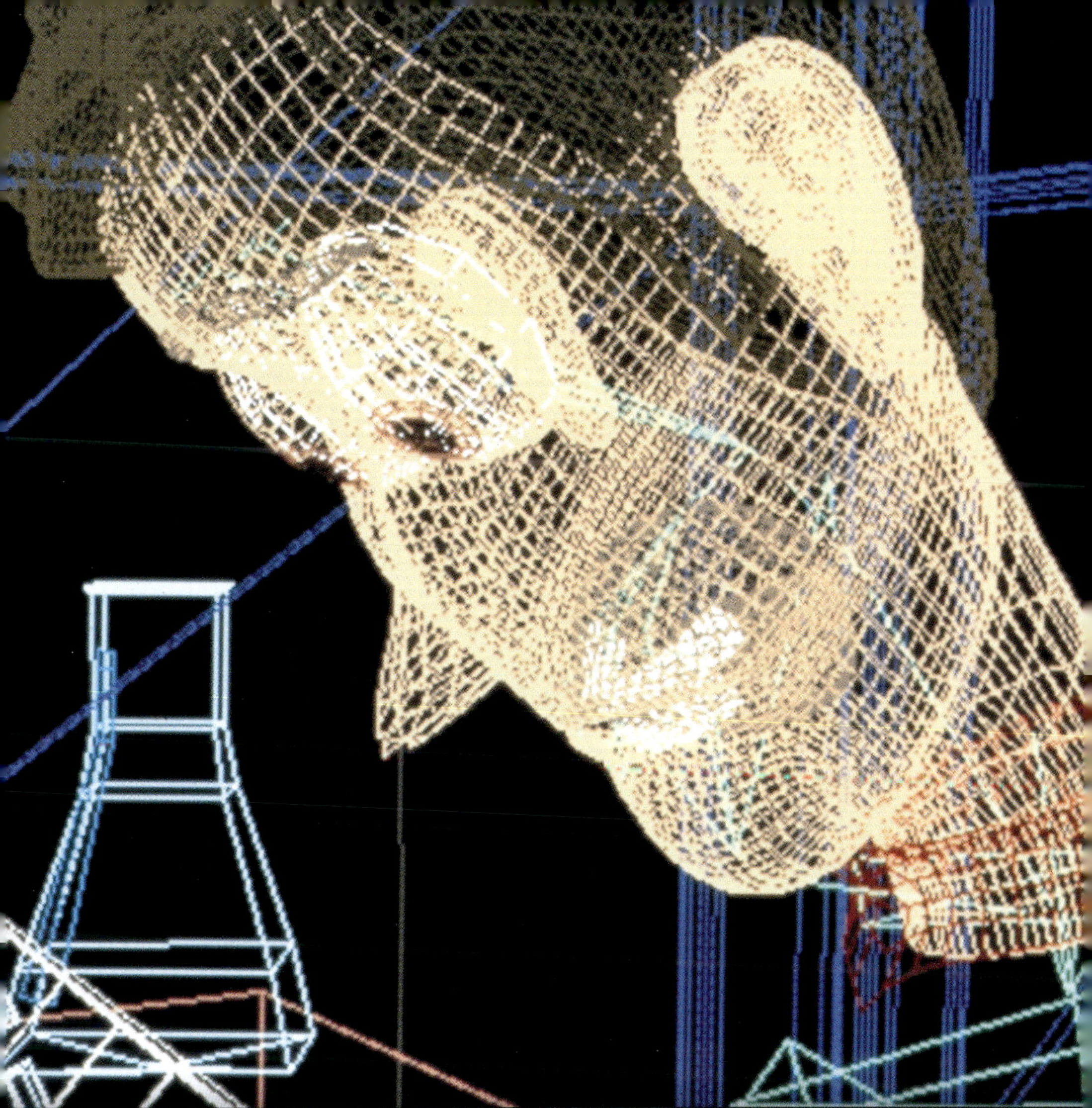

Animators had 117 computers running 24 hours a day. Each frame would take up to 30 hours to **render**. Pixar had to invent a new software, called Renderman, to handle all the animation.

Tom Hanks voiced Woody. Buzz Lightyear was voiced by Tim Allen. Because it was each of the stars' first time doing voice work, Hanks and Allen recorded Woody and Buzz's lines together.

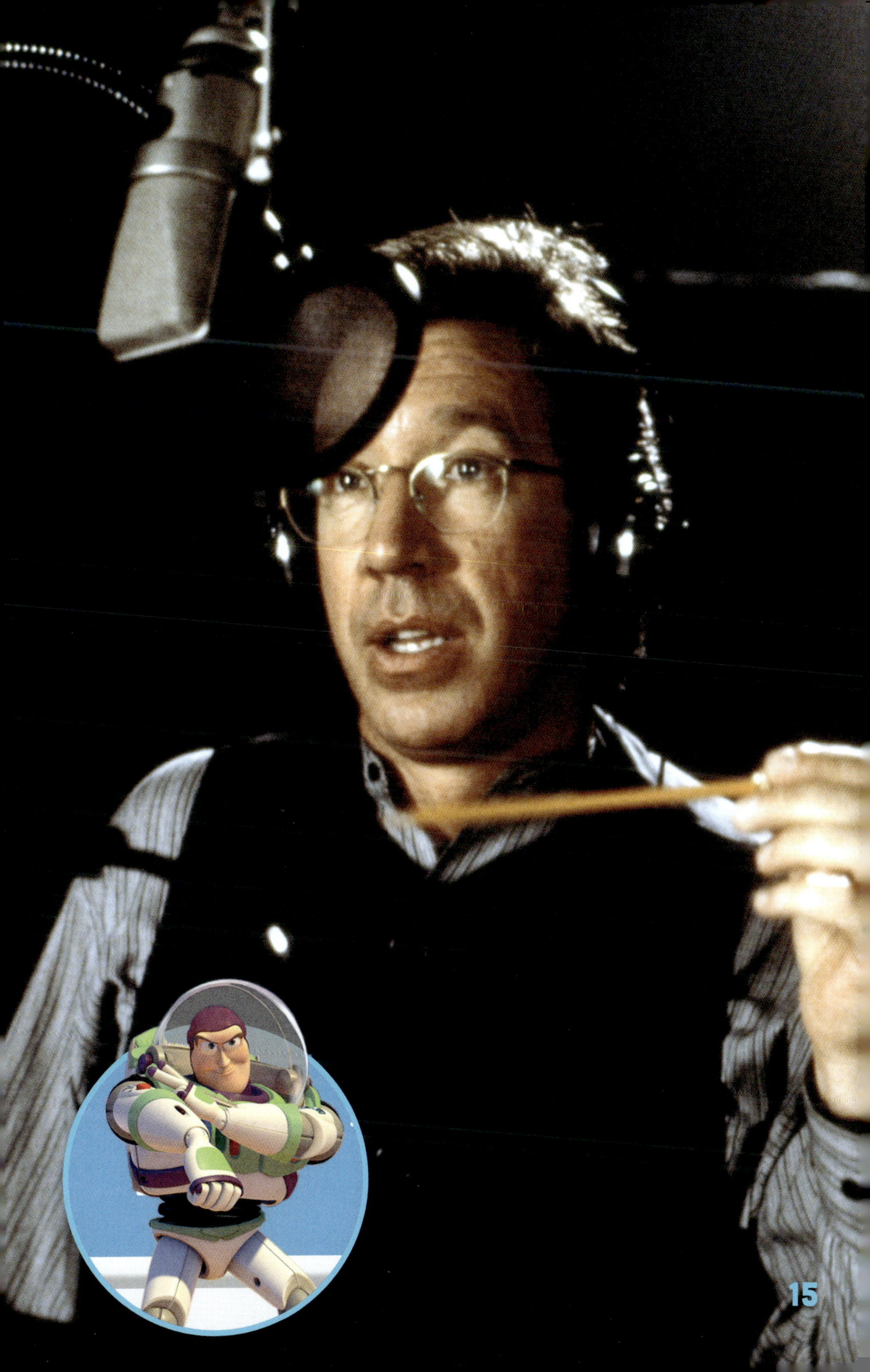

Disney wanted the film to be a musical. But Lasseter had a different vision. He brought in musician Randy Newman to create an original song. Newman wrote the **iconic**, “You’ve Got a Friend in Me” in one day.

Steve Jobs, head of Pixar at the time, thought *Toy Story* would fail. However, when Jobs saw the full movie, he knew that it would be a **milestone** in cinema history.

LEGACY

Toy Story was the highest **grossing** film of 1995. It was also the first animated film to be nominated for a Best Original Screenplay **Oscar**! *Toy Story* received a **Guinness World Record** as the first feature-length computer-animated film.

Three **sequels** were released in the years after. There have also been many shorts, video games, and real toys based on the film. *Toy Story* is a series that goes to infinity and beyond!

GLOSSARY

Academy Award – one of several awards the Academy of Motion Picture Arts and Sciences gives annually to achievement in the movie industry.

grossing – producing or earning an amount of money.

Guinness World Record – an award given to those who have broken a record not achieved by anyone else in the world.

hardware – the physical components that a computer system requires to function.

iconic – widely known or easily recognized.

milestone – an important event or turning point in a process or industry.

Oscar – another name for an Academy Award.

pitch – an idea for a movie by a screenwriter or producer.

render – the process of merging many different media files into a single file.

sequel – a movie or other work that continues the story begun in a preceding one.

ONLINE RESOURCES

Booklinks
NONFICTION NETWORK
FREE! ONLINE NONFICTION RESOURCES

To learn more about the making of *Toy Story*, please visit **abdobooklinks.com** or scan this QR code. These links are routinely monitored and updated to provide the most current information available.

INDEX